I0440118

Unfolding Identity:
Selected Stories from a Life

Jeffrey Zacko-Smith, Ed.D.

Printed in the United States of America

First Printing, 2015

ISBN: 978-1505556315

An Identity-Story Project Publication

www.identitystoryproject.com

This work is dedicated to several mentors without whom I might never have found my voice: Dr. John Gardiner at Seattle University; Dr. Roberto Pena at Seattle University; Dr. G. Pritchy Smith formerly of the University of North Florida; and Gail Wells and the National Coalition Building Institute (NCBI) Team at Buffalo State College. I am forever grateful.

"I am not a teacher, but an awakener."
~ Robert Frost

Preface

To say this book has been a work in progress would be an understatement. Though small, it began its life in 2007 as a chapter in a larger edited volume that was to be called *Leadership, Reform and Social Justice*, which was the idea of a graduate-school mentor. Though the book never materialized, the call to share my story[1] never diminished. In the intervening years, this work has been re-written, expanded, performed and shelved multiple times, and the sharing of my own story of identity has been both cathartic for me and, I think, helpful to others.

In 2010 I was fortunate to become affiliated with the National Coalition Building Institute (NCBI) while an Assistant Professor at the State University of New York College at Buffalo. The NCBI is an international non-profit leadership training organization based in Washington, DC, that, since its founding in 1984, has built global coalitions to help eliminate racism and all other forms of discrimination. An idea central to their diversity work, that happens to coincide with my own beliefs regarding individual identity (as well as the issues that develop when our identities are challenged) is that you don't change minds, you change hearts. ***How do you do*** *this? By sharing your own story.* Hearts don't respond to statistics. Thus, besides concepts refined through a decade of study, research, teaching, and the facilitation of diversity work, I'm sharing my own stories of identity, as well as how I have handled challenges to "who I am" throughout the years. I hope you find it meaningful.

People will forget what you said, they will forget what you did, but they will never forget how you made them feel.

~ Carl W. Buehner

This work is also part of a larger project called **The Identity-Story Project.** Every reader is hereby invited to share a story of their own related to identity on our website, and to use the affiliated resources to both educate themselves and others. Selected stories may be featured in an upcoming Identity-Story Project book.

Social change takes place in community, and powerful and authentic communities are facilitated by powerful and authentic individuals. Thinking about and sharing our individual stories of identity, and knowing that we have choices when our stories are challenged, is where change needs to begin. In her work *I Know Why the Caged Bird Sings* (1969), Maya Angelou wrote that "There is no greater agony than bearing an untold story inside of you." Be kind to yourself, share your story with the world and create change; visit our website at **identitystoryproject.com** to connect with our community and help us build coalitions one story at a time.

~ Jeffrey

So, the journey to Self is neither easy nor quick … but those who stay the course become the person they started out to be. They find their own voice, their own truth. Along the path, they not only understand their true Self but also claim their gifts, heed their call, move towards wholeness, and learn to be authentic.

~ R.S. Moxley

Our Quest

In today's world we are too often pushed to "find ourselves." And even worse yet, we're made to feel that we need to complete our exploration as soon as possible. How many of us have been told, in one way or another, that until we finish this journey we simply won't be authentic, interesting, inspirational to others or personally fulfilled? We're continually told that life is too short to be wasting time; we must reach our potential, and we must do it **NOW**. We are constantly prodded to "become everything that we can be", to find that space, time and place where we are fully "us." Once there, it is believed, we can venture forth to lead, to teach, to help and heal, to parent, to manage, and to move out into the world and make a difference.

Perhaps because of the language and images we're exposed to daily, we're led to believe that discovering our identity (note how the word "discovering" implies a degree of finality, as if we're searching for some long lost treasure, which, once found, will bring us everything we desire) is at worst some resting place, and at best some final destination after which nothing much is required of us, but possibility is limitless. **What if we chose differently?** What if we stopped and questioned the process of "becoming" that is pushed

upon many of us? Would our conceptions of identity, our ideas about

"who we are", hold up to close scrutiny, or would they be exposed as

partial truths … or even complete illusions?

Don't establish the
    boundaries
    first
    the squares, triangles,
    boxes
    of preconceived
    possibility,
    and then
    pour
life into them, trimming,
off left-over edges,
ending potential:
    let centers
    proliferate
    from
self-justifying motions.

~ A.R. Ammons (in Spears, 1998, p. 345)

Consider, just for a moment, that we have it all wrong. What if identity isn't a thing to be found, but is a journey; an unfolding of self-hood that neither begins nor ends, but unfurls behind, before and around us like a beautiful stretch of cloth made up of our lived experiences, our divinity, and our choices? Perhaps then, to use an all-too-true cliché, we could begin to appreciate the journey itself, and would spend much less time seeking the perfection that we, in fact, already possess in the now, just as we are. Since there would be no final destination to arrive at, any judgments about ourselves and others (since we would all be perfect as we are in each moment), and the ceaseless act of organizing our lives to such an extreme that we only truly succeed in killing the freedom, choice and creative power that we are trying to attain, would be pointless? When it comes to discovering who we are, can we ever cease learning, exploring, and discovering? Should we? Is there an end to the process? Is there an end to growth?

> ## In the world without foundations, everyone is equal and the imposition of any system of meaning on others is violence and oppression.

~ Gianni Vattimo (cited in Gergen, 1999, p. 222)

I've lived a life that has clearly shown me that, at any given time, a person can speak or act from a place that is only temporarily their own, and yet is the culmination of countless years and a myriad of experiences of both the good and the bad variety. **This "in the moment" self is the best that we can do.** It is also all that can be expected of us. Opinions, actions, ideas and beliefs are all contextual and based upon what has unfolded for each of us up to a very singular point in time, which is this moment, this "now." *How can it be any other way?* Thus, who we are, our identity, is not a missing piece meant to be "discovered" at all, but is a process meant to be experienced, appreciated, loved and accepted as it unfolds. *Ad infinitum.* As is often the case, we can only see the patterns (the events and relationships that have brought us to the place we're in at this moment in time) if given the opportunity for reflection. It is only then that we are able to realize how perfect we were and are just as we were and are; taking that realization with us as we unfold, continuing to move towards even more authentic being. There is immense power inherent in this unfolding since it is through acceptance that we become real, and it's through realness that our world is changed.

I don't understand why people care so much about showing that they are good; because I am rather comfortable with having badness, quite okay with being inexplicable. They tire themselves so. The light is beautiful; but light can't hide treasures like the darkness can.

~ C. Joybell C.

Knowing how I have come to be perfect as I am and in this moment is extremely valuable (and, ultimately, completely necessary) because one cannot truthfully live (and by implication, cannot truthfully lead, teach, manage, or be in relationship to any other person) without such knowledge. Living without knowing and accepting yourself as you are is equivalent to wearing a costume every moment of every day; it is always shallow, often cold, and mercilessly lonely. **Without authenticity, all of our relationships are tinged by fraud, and are never as meaningful and rewarding as they could be.** If you are ignoring life's call to you, if you're not seeking personal meaning and self-revelation, and if you're ignoring the fact that you are perfect as-is, you can easily damage us all.

Here's where this gets very personal. My own identity has been unfolding for as long as I can remember (I used to, after all, dress up and pretend that I was the Virgin Mary when I was 8 years old and alone in my bedroom; an innocent activity which was possibly foreshadowing, if examined using a psychoanalytic lens, my homosexuality and was also likely the result of my Catholic upbringing). Along the way, I have found that each new revelation, each new unfolding, has required several things in order to become real and meaningful for me; surrender, gentleness and an open heart. We must surrender to the idea that we are perfect as we are, and that we are where we're meant to be, and we must be gentle with ourselves in coming to terms with how we have "become", how we have unfolded and continue to unfold, without an end in sight. In large part, this means not taking the labels, the "shoulds" and the agendas that society sets for us all that seriously. We must also open ourselves to the possibility that the process has only just begun (whether we're 18, 46 or 70), and that, perhaps, there is no "end" to be realized. How comfortable are you with uncertainty? With ambiguity? With the unknown?

We shall not cease from exploration
And the end of all our exploring
Will be to arrive where we started
And know the place for the first time.
Through the unknown, unremembered gate
When the last of earth left to discover
Is that which was the beginning;
At the source of the longest river
The voice of the hidden waterfall
And the children in the apple-tree
Not known, because not looked for
But heard, half-heard, in the stillness
Between two waves of the sea.
Quick now, here, now, always—
A condition of complete simplicity
(Costing not less than everything)
And all shall be well and
All manner of thing shall be well
When the tongues of flame are in-folded
Into the crowned knot of fire
And the fire and the rose are one.

~ T.S. Eliot (1943)

The lesson of each new unfolding was only shown to me over time; and, not being a very patient person, there have been days when I wished that I could find that resting place, or, better yet, just be fully unfolded, having my potential realized. Game over. Ultimately though, if the process were this rushed, I would be forced to ask the question "what now?" The very nature of life is change, adaptation, death and rebirth. Not only is it unlikely that we could change this reality if we desired to, doing so would interrupt the process of our becoming, a process that is central to our humanity and to our survival.

While countless experiences and people (as well as personal awakenings) have influenced who I am in this moment, I can describe three general unfoldings that, when combined, resulted in the person now writing these words. These identities influence everything that I do and there is no aspect of my life that is untouched by them. These identities are transformations, and the start of transcendence. These identities are not destinations, labels, or descriptions, they are my unfolding self, and I cannot "be", would not become anything at all even remotely authentic, without understanding and accepting them with love. The unfolding has not always been easy, but I can now proudly say that I am queer, I am short, and I am Arab-American.

I. Queer

> We who lived in concentration camps can remember the men who walked through the huts comforting others, giving away their last piece of bread. They may have been few in number, but they offer sufficient proof that everything can be taken from a man but one thing: the last of the human freedoms -- to choose one's attitude in any given set of circumstances, to choose one's own way. ~ Viktor Frankl

"I love you and you will always be my son, but you know you are going to hell, don't you?" I sat in the kitchen chair too stunned to respond . . . my father on the other end of the phone 3,000 miles away. Yet I was also somehow completely unsurprised at hearing these words, which only served to prove that I knew the point to which my father's own identity had unfolded up to that time, and that I had witnessed the turns it had taken over the years. Sure, I knew plenty of *other people* who've heard such things (friends, old lovers, acquaintances), and I'd read about similar experiences in books and magazines (popular gay literature is full of dramatic and traumatic recountings of the coming out process). Yet, somehow it was never truly real for me, and it was too cliché and expected to actually ever happen, wasn't it? Really living through hearing these words is wholly different . . . and completely violating. And it's an experience that I would never wish to change even if I somehow could.

I had decided to tell my father that I was gay in 1996, even though this part of my identity unfolded for me years and years earlier (recall my love of the Virgin Mary – I ask you - what straight kid would ever pretend to be the mother of God, yet alone dress up to play the part?) and had been revealed to others in stages, garnering little fanfare, while I was in my 20's and early 30's. Having grown up in a somewhat conservative area of the Northeast (it was a small town really, filled with small town – but not bad or ill intentioned people - who had, in many cases, limited exposure to things that were outside what society told them was "normal"). Upon later reflection, it became clear that I left the place I grew up so that this part of my identity could unfold, and it was one of the greatest gifts that I ever gave myself. You see, we must sometimes make space for such things, and we cannot be afraid to give ourselves room to grow, to change, and to expand outward (and inward and upward and downward); this challenge is accurately described in the excerpt from Willy Wonka and the Chocolate Factory (1971) below. **Unfolding takes time. Unfolding takes space. Unfolding takes courage**. In the end, however, the gifts it brings are worthwhile and true.

> **Willy Wonka**: This is the great glass Wonkavator.
> **Grandpa Joe**: It's an elevator.
> **Willy Wonka**: No, it's a Wonkavator. An elevator can only go up and down, but the Wonkavator can go sideways, and slantways, and longways, and backways...
> **Charlie Bucket**: And frontways?
> **Willy Wonka**: ...and squareways, and front ways, and any other ways that you can think of. It can take you to any room in the whole factory just by pressing one of these buttons. Any of these buttons. Just press a button, and *zing*! You're off. And up until now, I've pressed them all... except one.
> [gestures to a button near the top of the Wonkavator]
> **Willy Wonka**: This one. Go ahead, Charlie.
> **Charlie Bucket**: Me?
> [Willy Wonka nods as Charlie presses the button]

One big question remained for me, though. What was I supposed to *do* with what my dad just told me? Should I let it destroy me (after all, my father said he believed I was going to hell because of something I *am*, something I have no choice in being, and something I am proud of being)? Should I completely ignore it, going on with my life as usual, pretending during my interactions with him that such a thing was never revealed, never heard? Should I hate him? Should I hate the fact that I was gay? Should I blame God, or my mother, or someone or something else? So. Many. Shoulds. What was I supposed to do (after all, we are led to believe that we must be active, that we must do something in situations like this, right)?

Ultimately, what I chose to do was learn[2]. That's right, ***I chose to learn.*** Sometimes when our identity is unfolding, we get to a point where we know that accepting a personal truth, completely and sincerely, is the only way we can continue to become who we are in the moment, and continue to become who we will be; such moments being one of many that make us authentic and whole. I felt great. Telling my father that I was gay was the final thing that I needed to do before allowing this part of my identity to fully emerge, and it was beautiful. It was real. It was necessary. It was painful.

Social justice starts with each of us as individuals (remember that authentically relating to others is directly related to authentically relating to self), and is moved along by the inner work that we do day in and day out (or, for others of us, just every so often). Living in a way that is socially just means, first and foremost, that we choose appropriately for ourselves, and take actions that bring us closer to our own authenticity. How can I expect to live authentically (and in my case lead and teach authentically) if I am hiding from myself?

II. Short

Even the smallest person can change the course of the future.
~ J.R.R. Tolkien

I know what it's like to be famous. Well, sort of, anyway. I know what it's like to walk into a room and immediately be the center of attention ("Wow! He's short!"), to be the object of speculation ("I wonder what's wrong with him?"), to be the object of assumption ("He must have a hard life."), and to delightfully surprise those around you, even those who know you the best, simply because you can endure ("I am so proud of the fact that you managed to accomplish *that*"). It's not so much that this kind of wonderment and curiosity is necessarily insulting, or that people mean to be hurtful or demeaning. I notice people who are "different" too. Unlike being gay, however, this unfolding was not something I could hide, it was noticeable and it was really not a big deal except on the days when it was. Of course having been 4'10" all of my adult life did, in some ways, prepare me for being gay; I was used to being a minority, used to being outside the "norm", and used to having to come to daily terms with being different.

I knew I was unique from as far back as I can remember. I was always shorter, skinnier, had the higher voice. I was always the "cute" one, which, again, isn't a bad thing, except for the times when you want to be taken seriously, or you want to feel sexy, or you want to be authoritative. What makes it all the more complicated is that I truly am unique (not that we all aren't unique in some way – but I'm being more literal here). The average height for an American man is 5'9" or so, and the cut off point for being a "little person" is known to be 4'9", depending on who you ask. I'm 4'10". I'm far from being of average height for my gender, and though close to being a "little person", not quite little enough. ***So, the question is, where do I fit in?*** Do I need to be categorized and labeled to be understood? Accepted? To feel good about myself?

Some of my most vivid childhood and teenage memories involve hospitals. My parents were, of course, concerned about my lack of growth, and so they did their best to investigate and make sure that nothing was wrong with me physically. I think, in some ways they were also worried about me "discovering" my identity; or, rather, discovering and then having to live with an identity that was outside society's mainstream. *Would I have a difficult life? Would I ever find someone to marry? What about school and career? Would I face discrimination?* The questions, as you can imagine, are truly endless, and seem so important, especially to a parent who loves their child, that they must have been somewhat overwhelming. In the end, as far as I know, the doctors simply said I was "short"; I didn't possess enough growth hormone to get me far enough, and 4'10" was it.

Now, it should be noted that, were I female, this would not really be as much of an issue. Sure, the average American female is about 5'3", and I'd still be undertall, but being a short woman is much more widely accepted. You see, being petite is associated with the feminine and not the masculine, at least in American culture (department stores even have separate departments for short women, but no such thing exists for men – and we all know if it's sanctioned by the retailers it's surely acceptable, surely normal – capitalism is the great equalizer. Yes, that is sarcasm). But, genes are genes, and my mom is short, my grandfathers and grandmothers were short, and my dad is the tall one at about 5'7". Genetically at least, being small was part of my physical destiny. It is also an unfolding that continues each and every day, and something I would not choose to change even if there was some way to suddenly become of average height.

Becoming a Person means that the individual moves toward being, knowingly and acceptingly, the process which he inwardly and actually is. He moves away from being what he is not, from being a façade. He is not trying to be security or bombastic defensiveness. He is not trying to be less than he is, with the attendant feelings of guilt or self-deprecation. He is increasingly listening to the deepest recesses of his psychological and emotional well-being, and finds himself increasingly willing to be, with greater accuracy and depth, that self which he most truly is.

~ Carl Rogers (1961, p. 176).

So here I am. Short. Much like the unfolding of my gay identity, the unfolding of my short identity left me with choices. I could give in to the thought that I could never have a normal life, that I would never be accepted. I could let my physical "limitation" hold me back, make me fearful, and keep me from taking risks. I could choose to be hurt by the stares, by the comments, by the assumptions that come along with the categories and labels that we assign one another. Or, I could choose to push forward, follow my dreams, and use what many would consider to be a handicap or a hardship to make a difference in my community and the world. I could use my own unfolding identity to become better, and to serve others.

I truly see my height (or lack thereof) as a gift now. Again, this was a revelation only bestowed on me through time and the opportunity for reflection. I would not be who I am in this moment or who I'll be in the future without the experiences I've had up to now. ***All of them are valuable, all of them are gifts.*** Recognizing that diversity is the nature of life itself requires knowing that one's uniquenesses are no better – nor worse – than any others. I find that I am more empathetic, more empathic, and a more caring and tolerant human being after developing genuine affection for the ways I am different. I appreciate diversity in ways I might not have otherwise. I look beyond the physical. I am a person who realizes that "normal" is simply an empty label, and this allows me to relate to and serve others more fully. Audre Lord, the great American poet, teacher and activist, is credited with saying "If I didn't define myself for myself, I would be crunched into other people's fantasies for me and eaten alive." The most powerful people we have in our lives should show us that our uniqueness is our strength, and they should encourage us to define ourselves for ourselves by serving as examples of what is possible, and by focusing on, valuing and honoring our authenticity.

III. Arab-American

Setting: Twelve year olds just after their summer break at a primarily white, upper-middle class Catholic elementary school having a conversation about what it must be like to be black and poor (there was only one black kid in our school as far as I knew, his name was Mike, and he got free tuition and free lunch every day, and was the object of much curiosity among the other students) in our primarily white middle-class community.

Debbie (one of my friends): "Well, ask Jeffrey, *he's* not poor but he is black."

Me: Silent. *Thinking to myself... "So, OK, if Debbie, who has known me for years, thinks I'm black, what do my other friends, or worse yet strangers, think about me"? Do they think about ME the way we seem to think about Mike? Not, of course, that I truly cared if people thought I was black (above and beyond feeling the pressure of wanting the unquestioned acceptance that most adolescents do), but if they were going to point out that I was different (in yet another way), they could at least get it right. What if they knew I liked guys and not girls, too? What then?*

My skin always was darker, especially after I came back to school from summer vacation. After weeks of swimming in the pool and going to the beach with my family, I would get very tan. Though I was only part Lebanese, those genetic traits dominated the other ethnicities (Irish, German, and French among them) in my family tree, and I always thought that I looked ethnic, much like my Middle-Eastern aunts and uncles, cousins and grandfather did. Plus, when I was younger I had very thick and dark curly hair, which I'm sure either made me look Latino, or perhaps even American Indian. But I certainly never considered that I looked black. The point is simple though; I did not look like the White Anglo-Saxon Protestants (or W.A.S.P.'s as they were referred to in my part of the world) that surrounded me at school. *Once again, I faced looking "different."* Not only was I short. Not only was I gay (though, admittedly, at twelve I was only out to myself), I looked *foreign.* Exotic. Unusual. My therapist told me recently that I looked like I was Egyptian, which was one ethnicity I hadn't ever considered. So, while my height (or lack thereof) certainly was the primary difference that people noticed and judged every day, the unfolding of my "foreign" identity certainly influenced my life in many ways.

For me, being foreign meant that I wasn't like everyone else in my community, and, to be truthful, I treasured that. Plus, that was easier to deal with than being short, anyway (I think "foreign" is generally seen as a more natural and normal label than is "short", which is often seen as a disability, another label that is troublesome for many reasons we will not explore). At least, as I alluded to before, looking foreign was seen as exotic in the small town of my childhood (not so much when I lived in larger cities), and, perhaps, especially to a young kid, it was somewhat fun and mysterious to be looked at that way. I always felt closer to the Lebanese side of my family, partly because they were "different" too – loud, kind of crazy, completely stubborn, and very proud in a down to Earth sort of way. In retrospect, I know that I was lucky; I personally never experienced discrimination (at least not that I know of) based on heritage, though

I certainly did hear the term "crazy Arab" muttered about someone in my family now and then. Lucky for me, I thought crazy was cool!

After traveling to the Mediterranean in my 30's, I decided to self-identify as Lebanese-American, and I added the Zacko (my mom's maiden name and Lebanese grandfather's last name) to the much more common Smith. Doing this just seemed "right," just seemed necessary. Have you ever been somewhere and felt very distinctly that you'd been there before – that the place and the people were, somehow, infused into your own DNA – that they were a part of your being, part of your true self? This is exactly how I felt when I finally spent time in France and Italy and Greece (which is as close as I have yet come to the Middle East). Being in these places felt much better than being at "home" ever did – it felt more natural, and I felt more alive and connected somehow – even though I had no immediate or recent ties to the culture, people or landscape. I choose, now more than ever, to celebrate my Middle-Eastern heritage, and to let it shape me in every way that I can.

Making Meaning

As citizens in today's post-modern, post-industrial world, we are confronted with the need to embrace diversity in unprecedented ways. Our ability to remain culturally, sexually, racially, religiously and ideologically isolated is at an end whether we like it or not. Personally, I find it exciting. But, living in such times requires that we first achieve some level of acceptance of our own truth; acknowledging (and loving) our own unfolding self. **This is never easy.** It is, however, required if we desire to live authentically; how can we embrace the diversity that surrounds us if we can't fully accept, appreciate and grow from our own? This is our challenge.

In our increasingly globalized society, in communities that are hyper-diverse and require us to exhibit patience, flexibility, empathy and understanding simply to function in socially just ways, we need people who, first and foremost, are comfortable with how they are different, and who can celebrate the differences that exist all around them, using those differences as the gifts that they are. "Finding ourselves" should never be seen as a goal and should not be an end-point or resting place; it should be an ongoing process of unfolding and a continual appreciation of our identities. I'm brought back to words written by Audre Lord, who stated "It is not our differences that divide us. It is our inability to recognize, accept, and celebrate those differences." Allowing our identity to unfold and telling our own story is a great place to begin.

Facing Challenges

The ideas presented in the pages of this book are not intended to make it seem as if allowing our identity to unfold is easy; nor is facing those people and circumstances that challenge us and our understanding of who we are. **Ultimately I believe that what we are called to do is simply realize that we have choices.** We have the choice to accept ourselves (though this is always a process that takes time); we have the choice to accept others; and we have the choice to learn and grow when we are faced with people and ideas that want to oppress or marginalize us. As Maya Angelou's (1978) words allude to on the following page, we always have the choice to rise.

You may shoot me with your words,
You may cut me with your eyes,
You may kill me with your hatefulness,
But still, like air, I'll rise.

References

Angelou, M. (1978). *And still I rise.* New York: Random House.

Angelou, M. (1969). *I know why the caged bird sings.* New York: Random House.

Eliot, T.S. (1943). *The four quartets.* San Diego: Harcourt, Inc.

Gergen, K. (1999). *An invitation to social construction.* London: Sage Publications.

Marguiles, S. & Wolper, D. (Producers), & Stuart, M. (Director). (1971). *Willy Wonka & the chocolate factory* [motion picture]. United States: Paramount Pictures.

Rogers, C. (1961). *On becoming a person.* Boston: Houghton Mifflin.

Spears, L., (Ed.). (1998). *Insights on leadership.* New York: John Wiley and Sons.

End Notes

1. This is primarily a story book versus an academic work; therefore some creative license has been exercised in the writing, wording and arrangement of this material.

2. My relationship with my father has evolved over the years, and I know he loves me and I love him. This story was told to capture a moment in time and my own perception of an experience and does not reflect a current state. Identities evolve, and time heals.

About the Author

Jeffrey David Zacko-Smith is a writer, diversity trainer and faculty in Organizational Leadership at Colorado State University's Global Campus. He is also adjunct faculty at Black Hills State University in South Dakota, where he teaches a course on diversity and social change. For 5 years he was Assistant Professor of Leadership and Creative Studies, as well as Coordinator of the undergraduate Leadership Minor Program, at Buffalo State College in Buffalo, NY, where he also served as Interim Director of Leadership Development (2012-2013).

Jeffrey holds both a Doctorate in Educational Leadership (Ed.D.) and a Master of Public Administration (M.P.A.) Degree from Seattle University, as well as both a B.A. in Industrial Psychology and an A.A. in Writing from Penn State University, plus numerous certifications.

The author has been teaching leadership, diversity and multiculturalism, and social change for years, receiving two Faculty Appreciation Awards from Buffalo State for his inclusive classroom practices. His research, writing and activism are focused on multiple areas, including building authentic, transcendent and diversity-conscious leaders, social constructionism, and exploring issues of identity.

Jeffrey has presented his writing and research at numerous national and international conferences and workshops (2005-2015), has published in the *Leadership Review*, *Academic Exchange Quarterly*, and *Multicultural Education*, co-authored several book chapters, as well as authored an entry in the *Encyclopedia of Diversity in Education* and a monograph on Constructionist Leadership.

His doctoral dissertation, *The Leader Label,* was classified as "noteworthy" by the internationally known Taos Institute due its contribution to the field of Social Constructionism. He is a trainer affiliated with the National Coalition Building Institute and has been working to address issues of leadership oppression, racism and social justice in organizations and communities.

Dr. Zacko-Smith is available for speaking engagements and to facilitate workshops and learning around diversity and inclusion, issues of identity, diversity leadership, and general leadership development. **Connect with him!** jzackosmith@gmail.com

About The Cover

The image used on the book cover was taken by the author in Buffalo, NY, and was chosen for its symbolism. Though identity is rooted in self, over time it grows, climbs and reaches outward, always bright and colorful and continually receiving support from the diverse world in which it both exists and from which it draws its strength. Diversity is life itself. May we all recognize its gifts!

About the Photos

1. Cover – Abandoned Warehouse & Vines, Buffalo, New York.
2. Page 8 – A shop in Downtown Durham, North Carolina.
3. Page 11 – "Demon" Wheat Paste Art, Buffalo, New York.
4. Page 17 – Virgin Mary statue, Key West Cemetery, Key West, Florida.
5. Page 19 – "Love" Mural – Downtown Buffalo, New York.
6. Page 30 – The author as a child in Pennsylvania.
7. Page 34 – Interior, Reims Cathedral, Reims, France (stained glass windows by Marc Chagall).

www.ingramcontent.com/pod-product-compliance
Lightning Source LLC
Chambersburg PA
CBHW040327010626
45792CB00024B/2225